Few people will ever visit a children's hospital in Africa, but Elaine's impressionistic style of writing and storytelling opens a window into that world. Here, a reader who is considering humanitarian or volunteer service will find both sobering reality and moments of joy, often in the same story. These true, personal accounts will be valuable resources for individuals who are new to missions or relief work. For myself, even after many years of serving in a missions capacity, these essays prompted me to remember that whatever we do in service to the King, real change is made one relationship at a time. Elaine's writing reveals the beauty and wonder of that truth.

Hope Carter, PA, MHSc
Moffat Bible College
Kijabe, Kenya

The first sentence of each chapter lured me into reading all of the stories without stopping. With transparency and candor, Elaine shared her story and bared her heart. This allows us all to live the experience with her—the pain and joy of following Christ in a hard place.

Millie Bransford
Bethany Children's Hospital
Kijabe, Kenya 1998-2015

———

Entering into another's suffering is a bold undertaking. This is especially true in a cross-cultural setting where the limitations of our own wisdom and experience are ever before us. I am struck by Elaine's courageous prayer that she might take upon herself the pain of another person and even experience that pain on their behalf. If compassion really means "to suffer with", these true stories are beautiful examples of that willingness to share in the suffering of another. To engage repeatedly in such a challenging setting is uniquely to "Bear one another's burdens and so fulfill the law of Christ."

Kristopher Hartwig, MD
Family Medicine, Hospice and Palliative Care
13 years serving in Tanzania

"I Am Sho-Sho, too" is Elaine Brautigam's account of her volunteer service as a chaplain at Bethany Kids Children's Hospital in Kijabe, Kenya. Admittedly unprepared and inexperienced, Elaine soon discovers her gift of observation and storytelling. In this brief memoir she shares stories of healing wounds of the body and wounds of the spirit. We enter Kijabe, a place of compassion, a place where people love and comfort one another even in the hardest of times. We enter a place where "the night sky is ablaze with stars and the moon is so bright it casts a shadow." We enter a place where no one suffers alone.

Justus M. Marete, CEO
Maua Methodist Hospital
Maua, Kenya

Through personal story telling, Elaine shares her experiences of volunteering alongside the chaplain at a children's hospital in Kenya. With care, humility and wit, her journal entries introduce us to the children and their caregivers. Themes of interdependence, commonality, generosity of spirit, forgiveness and hope appear as well as irony, disappointment and sadness. The vignettes cut through race, language and social standing, exposing not only human suffering, but caring and rewarding work in faithful Christian service. A treasure shared, this collection is easy to read but carries a depth of understanding valuable for anyone who has worked or hopes to serve in a culture not one's own.

Rebecca Hartwig, RN, DNP
Missionary nurse and educator, Tanzania

I AM SHO-SHO, TOO

I AM SHO-SHO, TOO

An African Memoir

ELAINE BRAUTIGAM

 Created with Vellum

Contents

For Mercy,

"I want to be faithful. I have a choice, and I choose to be faithful. My Lord Jesus was faithful. He hung on that cross and was faithful. He could say, 'No! I am getting down from the cross. I want to go home for tea.' But no, He hung there and died for my sins. He was faithful, and I will be faithful to Him."

-Mercy Ng'ang'a, Pediatric Chaplain, Bethany Kids Hospital Kijabe, Kenya, 2017

All proceeds from the sales of this book will be donated to Bethany Kids Children's Hospital in Kijabe, Kenya.

Introduction

Backstory

Most people sent out by World Medical Mission are doctors. They are physicians of every conceivable medical specialty with impressive credentials and valuable, marketable skills. They leave their own practices or come out of retirement to volunteer in underserved locations around the world. My husband, Don, a family physician, took a ten-week sabbatical to serve as a short-term medical missionary at Kijabe and Bethany Kids Hospital in Kenya. This was to be our fifth such trip to Africa, the third to this particular hospital.

During the planning stage of our short-term missions trip, I was often asked what I would be doing in Africa. A reasonable question deserved a reasonable answer. Unfortunately, I didn't have one. Clearly, in America we are a nation of "doers," and I, too, felt the need for a mission, a job, an identity to justify the long and expensive trip we were about to take. But I didn't have one. I had been assured there was certain to be "something for me to do."

As our departure drew near, I found peace and encouragement in Ephesians 2:10, where the apostle Paul writes, "For we are God's workmanship, created in Christ Jesus to do good works, which God prepared in advance for us to do." I left the U.S. with some apprehension, but also with the expectation that God's "work" for me was prepared in advance, and when the time was right, it would be made clear.

Upon arrival at Kijabe Hospital, I began to assist the Bethany Kids Pediatric Chaplain, Mercy Ng'ang'a. Timidly at first, I walked through the wards, visiting and praying with each young patient and the parent who stayed with the child. I was embarrassed about my halting, self-conscious prayers. But God grew in me a deep affection for the children and their parents. God showed me that my awkwardness was not a hindrance to the Holy Spirit. Most of all, I could see I was doing the very work He prepared in advance for me.

Over time, I began to desire that I might take their pain upon myself and experience it on their behalf. Could they, in turn, experience the relief of having someone else, me, carry their pain, their fear, their sadness, for a while? Could they step aside to rest, sleep or pray in peace while another took their place? I don't know how that happened, but I think, on occasion, it did.

Although the patients' names have been changed to protect their privacy, their stories are true. I wrote them so I could settle my racing mind from rehearsing and replaying the scenes, the people and the sadness in my head. The people really exist, the events really happened, and the experience has changed me forever.

ONE

I Am Sho-Sho, Too

_____

Kijabe, Kenya, first Monday

OUR TEMPORARY HOME IS COLD. Sterile. Tile floor. Tile ceiling. One light bulb per room. Metal bars in the windows. Metal gate at the door. What dangers in this place are so threatening that they necessitate the presence of a metal gate on our door? Do I really need a metal gate to protect me from... Kijabe?

Can a metal gate protect my heart?

A woman about my age has come to help me clean the house. I don't need her help. I don't want her help. Not today. Not tomorrow. Not next week. I can clean my own house.

But this is her job. I don't need her, but she needs me.

On the table, she sees the picture of my family at home in America.

She pauses. "These are your... grand-chil-dren?" She pronounces this big word so clearly and carefully that my own grandchildren might not understand that she is talking about me, "Grammy."

But I say, "Yes. These are my grandchildren."

She studies the picture. "You are grand-moth-er. In Kikuyu we say, 'Sho-Sho.' It is much easier to say 'Sho-Sho.' You are Sho-Sho. I am Sho-Sho, too...We are the same."

Kijabe, week two

The same woman comes to the door. "Next week my grandson goes back to school. He leaves on Monday. It is the beginning of a new term, and I need money for his school fees. I have no one to help pay the fees, but my grandson needs an education, or... or... he will be like me. Sho-Sho, can you help?"

Voices of experienced people fill my head, admonishing me, almost scolding me: Do not give money to local people. It will make them dependent. It will encourage them to ask for more.

I look at my husband, who looks away. I look at my string bag on the table. It holds my notebook, my pencil, my house key and my wallet. I look at the Sho-Sho at the door; she waits in silence; I imagine her voice praying loudly in her head. I say, "I will think about it. Come back Monday."

And, for now, I close the door on her need.

Kijabe, week four

I am in the hospital ward. Ten metal beds, five on each side of the room. In each bed is a child and next to that child, an adult watching. It is quiet for a room of ten children and their adults. I speak to each, shake hands with all, even the infants. Privately, I visit each bedside. We talk and pray so quietly that only we and God can hear.

The last bed is empty, linens slept in, yet unmade. In the chair an elderly lady sits silently, not looking, not moving.

I pause in front of her; standing close, I say, "Mama, where is the child in this bed?" She says something softly, but not in English. I try again.

"Mama," I say, pointing to the bed, "where is the child who sleeps here?" She repeats herself, but I don't understand.

I sit on the bed and reach to hold her hand. Our voices are low, and I lean forward to hear her better, my voice uncertain and halting.

"But Mama," I say, "where is the child?"

Now, as I anticipate her answer, tears begin to fill my eyes. The old woman looks up and our eyes meet. Her own pool of tears spill onto her soft, aged cheeks. Her grip on my hand tightens. There is another long pause, and then she speaks.

"The child is no more. The child is gone, and I was her Sho-Sho."

TWO

Matthew

─────────────

JUST UP THE road from our house in Kijabe is a
path to the hospital. Alongside the path is a clearing
in the brush. This is where the neighborhood
garbage cans are kept.

Actually the place looks like a garbage can cage.
Several times a week, each household dumps its
garbage in the cans kept in that enclosure. It's made
of wire fencing about eight feet long by six feet wide,
and quite tall. There is a wire roof on it.

Dog proof.

Monkey proof.

It seems that people are not particular about
actually getting their garbage into the cans. To do so
would require them to open the door and step into
the cage. Tossing their garbage in the general direc-

tion of the cans must be good enough, though, because a good portion of the mess ends up scattered and piled up all around the target cans.

In my mind's eye, I imagine nine-year-old boys being asked to take out the garbage. If I had a nine-year-old boy, I feel quite sure it would be his job. And I feel quite sure the accuracy of his aim would reflect the speed with which he wanted to complete the task.

One day, I was walking to Bethany Kids Hospital, and there was a person in the garbage cage. A grown man. In most African households, this would probably be the person least likely to be seen there.

As I approached him, I saw he was sorting garbage and thoughtfully filling containers according to their kind: food scraps here, paper there, recyclables in this bag.

Earlier in the day, I had walked by and noted to myself what a disgusting mess it was. I had wished somebody would "do something."

So here he was, only a few hours later, doing this very thing. He was not finished, but it was a remarkable improvement.

I stopped to speak to him. I thanked him for making the neighborhood so much nicer, for tackling such a disgusting, thankless job.

He paused and stood up straight. From crouching on the ground to standing adult height was quite a trip. He was well over six feet tall and built for hard work. He wore overalls and his rubber gloves reached his elbows.

After a brief pause, he spoke perfect English to me with authority and conviction.

"It 'tis my job. It 'tis my calling," he said simply.

I stood speechless.

"It 'tis humble work, but I do it for my Lord Jesus Christ." I could hardly believe my ears. "There are many people at Kijabe Hospital doing different jobs. They are following God's leading in their lives. This is where He has called me, and I have joy in my work."

I found my words and said, "What you are doing is important, and it makes a big difference to those who live and work here that you are so conscientious."

His response: "I do it for the Lord."

He shifted his weight and looked down briefly. Then he lifted his head and shared his thoughts:

"Maybe someday, someone will say, 'That man, Mathew, he is a good worker. He stays late to finish the job and does not complain. We should reward him with a better job.' That may happen someday, but maybe not. Maybe God is the only one who sees what I do, but if He sees me and He is pleased, that is all I ask.

"I get tired, but I remind myself, 'The joy of the Lord is my strength!' and I am renewed."

His words shook me to the core, and I had a sense that I was in the presence of a truly Godly man. Here, I thought, is a man who lives his life in the shadows. Yet he will surely have a place of dignity and honor in the upside-down Kingdom of God which is to come.

THREE

Rachel

A STANDARD HOSPITAL room in the pediatric ward contains ten beds for ten children. Each adult sleeps alongside, in the same bed as the child.

By comparison, around the corner are four less-frequently-used smaller rooms that comfortably hold just two beds.

Typically, these rooms are for patients isolated from the others for infection control, or wealthy patients who pay extra for the "private ward."

These few rooms around the corner are the last ones I come to on my daily rounds. I admit, I sometimes skip this section. Often, by the time I get there, the patients' lunch of beans and maize is being served. They are eating, and I am drained. I call it a day.

To my shame, I have been known to neglect them.

One Monday morning, in the private ward, a woman sat on the bed, her child sleeping next to her. She must have been admitted over the weekend because the room had been unoccupied the previous Friday.

The child's mother was stunning. She had perfect posture, and her head was held high, with a slight turn of the chin. Her back was straight with her feet on the floor. Despite the faded pink hospital gown the mothers were required to wear, she managed to project the calm and dignified presence of royalty.

Her legs were crossed at the ankles and slanted to the side. Her hands were quietly folded in her lap, and she was looking through the ajar door directly at me in the hall.

When our eyes locked, she gave a slight but definite smile. It was as if she recognized me or was expecting me and I had finally arrived.

I felt about 50 percent trapped and 50 percent intrigued.

Walking into the room, I could see she was younger than I'd thought. She looked like a teenage girl, but even that age didn't seem quite right. Her beauty was more refined than that of a pretty teenage girl. She was young but had such a quiet peace about her, I realized I was even a little intimidated.

When I meet the moms, I try to adapt to the way they present themselves to me. If I get a hearty handshake and a big smile, I give a hearty handshake and big smile in return.

I approach a very shy mom with my head bowed

and sit close to her on the bed or even kneel, so I am looking up to her.

If someone acts hostile, I approach her slowly and offer my hand, saying, "Can I sit with you and talk for a minute?"

I had no idea what to do with this young woman. What was it about her that had me so unglued?

She rose to meet me. This never happens. She extended her arm to shake my hand, and we stood facing one another. I asked her several "ice breaker" questions:

"What is your name?"

Pause.

"What is your baby's name?"

Pause.

"When did you come to Kijabe Hospital?"

Pause.

She calmly looked me in the eyes with a pleasant expression but didn't say a word. She didn't act flustered or uncomfortable. She just said nothing.

This really puzzled me. Primary school goes through eighth grade and is free in Kenya. Surely, she finished primary school and could speak conversational greetings. She was old enough to have attended high school as well. This would require tuition, or "school fees" as they are called, and she appeared to be from a prosperous family.

Kenyans place great value on education, and teaching is a highly esteemed profession. I didn't think money would stand between this elegant young woman and a good education.

Still trying to put the pieces together, I asked, "Do you speak English?"

A simple "No English," answered the question but didn't get me any closer to understanding the mystery which surrounded her. I clearly had no idea how to proceed.

Many people who don't speak English can still understand it a little, even if they are reluctant to use the little they have.

I held my hands in a praying position and asked her, "Pray?"

She nodded "Yes" and clasped her hands together.

I cupped my hands together, covering hers. We bowed our heads together and prayed. At the end, she echoed my "Amen."

Still holding hands, we looked at each other and smiled. As I started to leave, she pulled me back by the hand. Then she removed the thickly beaded Maasai bracelet which was on her arm. She smiled and held it out.

"For me?" I said.

She nodded, "Yes."

Holding the bracelet in my hand, I spoke slowly. "I cannot take this. It's beautiful, but I cannot take this."

She pushed my hand away and pulled me into her world. "For you."

Tears stung my eyes. "Thank you. Asante. Asante Sana."

Swallowing hard, I took her hand in mine for a moment, blinking away tears. "Thank you. Asante. Goodbye."

FOUR

Hope

———————

WHEN GEORGE'S mother abandoned him, his father left him with his grandmother because he could not work and take care of the boy.

While George was in the care of his grandmother, he and a friend were outside playing and riding bicycles. As the boys were racing down a road, George darted out on to a busy highway and was hit by a car. He received serious orthopedic injuries to his legs and traumatic brain injuries.

After the accident, George was admitted to Bethany Kids Hospital, where he was treated for his orthopedic injuries. The father's cousin, Hope, became his hospital guardian. She took over all his personal care needs. He was left immobile, in bed, without the ability to speak, feed himself, drink, dress himself or use the toilet.

When I arrived at Bethany Kids, George's orthopedic injuries had been treated, and he was receiving physical therapy. However, he resisted and cried out when a therapist tried to get him even to bend or straighten his limbs.

The head injuries continue to be an issue. He grimaces, looks tortured, holds his limbs rigid and twisted. Up until a few weeks ago, his body would tremor and move spasmodically. That has improved a little, but his arms and legs are still quite rigid and not easily manipulated.

Hope is concerned he is not getting enough to eat. He is extremely thin and resists eating. She has been augmenting his diet by spoon-feeding him diluted yogurt.

Hope is devoted to George and his care. I have never seen her feel sorry for herself or regret undertaking this responsibility.

Before this event, she lived in a resort city on the coast where she worked in a pharmaceutical business, packing medical supplies for shipping. She has a nine-year-old daughter, whom she left with a neighbor while she tends to George during his hospitalization and recovery.

This young woman made a decision to stay with her cousin's son and take care of every need and detail of his life. She seems to give no thought to her own comfort or convenience. Even now, ten weeks into his hospitalization, she is upbeat and optimistic about George's future. She is unwaveringly committed to the task of rehabilitating and retraining him, to whatever degree he is capable.

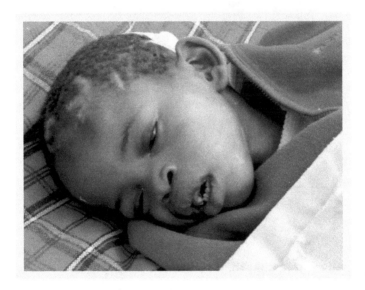

I doubt Hope has ever considered whether the sacrifice was worth it.

When I asked her about that very issue, she paused to think, then continued:

"Why should I complain? I am doing what I have said I would do. George is doing better. He is not well yet, but I can't give up on him. He is getting better. It would be ugly to leave him, and how can I be ugly? I am doing the right thing. How can I be ugly?"

One week prior to my departure, I entered the pediatric ward to a puzzling sight. Hope was slowly walking backwards down the corridor. As I drew nearer, I saw George holding her hands and standing before her.

With great care and concentration, Hope was guiding him as he took tentative steps down the hall.

George's traumatized brain was talking to his body, and his atrophied muscles responded to his will. George was healed.

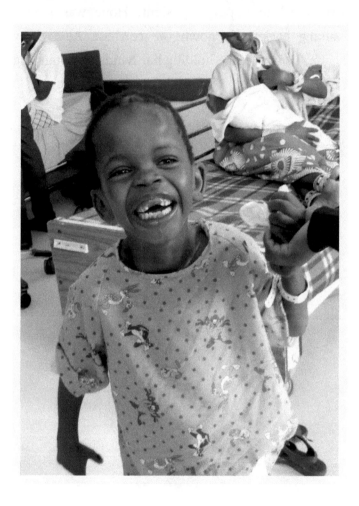

FIVE

Elizabeth

_____

SUCH A LITTLE GUY.

Ethan was born at seven months gestation. Now, two months later, he is still... such a little guy.

His Mama is a very pretty young woman. She is slender with delicate features. She smiles reluctantly and speaks in a quiet voice. She does not socialize with the other women on the ward. But she does what the nurses tell her to do, as they coax her to feed her baby. So much advice.

"He doesn't stay on the breast long enough."

"Try this" and "Try that" they urge.

She tries expressing her milk into a tube to feed him with a syringe. That does not seem to work, either.

"Perhaps she gives up too easily."

Elizabeth is aloof and hard to reach. She had little to say to me. She "let" me pray for her and the baby, but she didn't seem too invested in the prayer.

At first, she reminded me of a spoiled teenager: sullen, uncommunicative and bored. But as days turned into weeks, I saw her passivity turn into frustration, and then discouragement and defeat.

One day on my visit, I told her that I have a grandson who is also named Ethan. It was as if I had hit a nerve. She raised her head and looked straight at me. "Do you have a picture of your Ethan?"

"Why, yes, I do!" I said.

The next day, I brought her the picture of "my Ethan." She thinks he is very handsome. Delicately holding the print, she examined the picture carefully. Then the questions poured out, one fast on the heels of the other. No time for thought, no time for conversation. Just question after question, showing insatiable curiosity about the little boy whose picture she held in her hands.

Over several days, I shared more details about my Ethan. A little more information for her each day.

"My Ethan plays ball."

"My Ethan likes to run."

"My Ethan likes to read stories."

Then one day, "My Ethan got a guinea pig for Christmas."

"A WHAT?"

"A guinea pig!" I said.

"He got a PIG for Christmas???" So, we got that straightened out.

The next day she had a few questions about pets.

"Why didn't he get a cat or a dog for Christmas?"

"Well," I said, "they have a cat, but it's a family cat. The guinea pig is just for him."

Pause. "That was a good idea."

She nods.

Little by little, she opened up more. Never one for a lot of words, but she showed curiosity about a little boy in America who likes to run and play games. And he got a guinea pig for Christmas. His name is Ethan, just like her very little boy in the bassinet next to her.

Will he make it? Will he grow up to run and play games?

Maybe for Christmas, she'll get him a guinea pig.

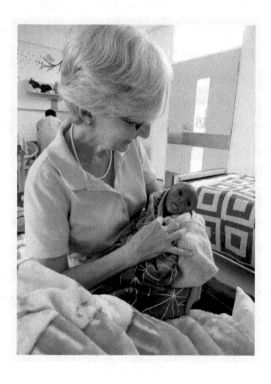

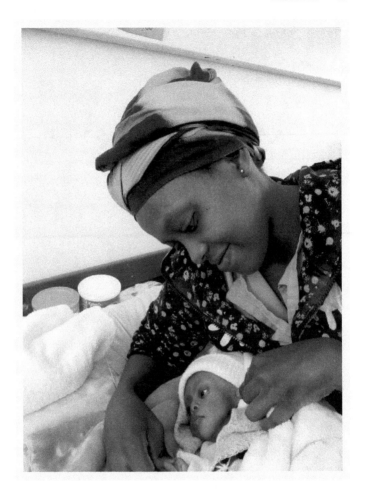

SIX

Ann

AT THE END of the hall, last room on the left, was
Ann. She was older than most of the pediatric
patients, maybe twelve or thirteen. Her mother often
neglected her responsibilities as a caregiver. She had
a habit of wandering off, away from the ward, for
long periods of time to unknown locations.

Yet Ann sat there, day after day, bolt upright,
alone, on the edge of the bed, her face frozen in a
wide, grimacing smile. She sat, staring straight ahead
with that fixed, maniacal smile. Every time I came
into the room, we had the same conversation.

She proclaimed in a loud, shrill, unexpressive
voice, "I AM GOING HOME TODAY!"

"Oh, that's wonderful, Ann! You must be so
happy."

"YES! I AM SO VERY HAPPY TODAY! FOR TODAY I AM GOING HOME!"

There was little variety in our daily "conversation." If I asked a question, I got the same bold declaration that she was going home today. The fact that she always wore street clothes instead of a hospital gown gave credence to her insistence, day after day, that yes, perhaps she really was going home "today."

But instead of becoming accustomed to this peculiar girl, I began to find her menacing. I became increasingly unglued by her odd behavior and appearance. Early on, I had been judgmental about her mother's wandering away. But I began to feel like wandering away myself.

In all the many days Ann sat there proclaiming her imminent departure, I never knew why she was in the hospital.

I never actually met her mother, but I am told that one night, quite late, her mother became floridly psychotic. She was going through alcohol withdrawal and began thrashing about and tearing up the hospital room. She was so violent that she had to be subdued and removed from the ward.

By the time I got there the next day, the mother had been replaced by another woman who took no more interest in Ann than the first mother had.

One day, soon after the arrival of the new mother, when I entered Ann's room, she gave me her usual greeting, then added, "PLEASE GIVE ME A GIFT THAT WILL REMIND ME OF YOU."

"Oh, Ann, that's wonderful that you are going home today. But I have no gift for you."

"I CAN WAIT WHILE YOU GO TO YOUR HOUSE TO GET SOMETHING."

Caught off guard, I said, "Yes, Ann... I will do that."

I came back later with a small object: a pen, a hair ribbon, or bar of scented soap... something small and "pre-teenish."

She accepted the gift but seemed to have forgotten asking for it. She did tell me again that she was going home today, in just a little while.

And that day, she did.

SEVEN

Caleb

MOST OF THE TIME, the mother or another female family member accompanies a child for the duration of his or her hospital stay.

This day, I walked into the ward and a child about seven years old sat on the bed next to a young man who was an appropriate age to be his father. I introduced myself to the child, and he told me his name was Martin.

He said the name, carefully articulating the "t" so it sounded like Mar-Tin. Very Kenyan.

He had bandages on both hands that looked like gauze boxing gloves. I patted him on the shoulder as a form of greeting, not wanting to make too big a deal of an infirmity that probably causes him a good bit of teasing. They really did look like boxing gloves.

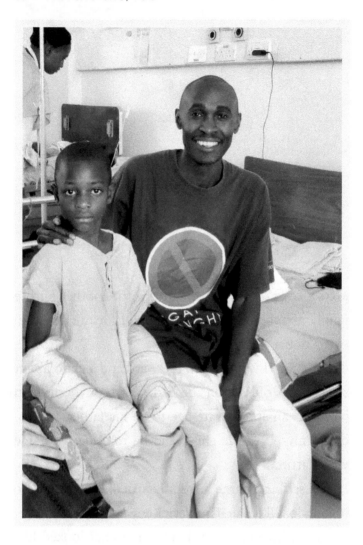

Turning my attention to his "father," I realized once again that I am not a very good guesser. Not the dad.

I had him pegged as an athlete. I guessed right

this time.

I later found out he was a Kenyan long-distance runner. Although he played down that aspect of his life, my clandestine internet search revealed a man of considerable success in the field of competitive running.

Over the weeks that Martin was a patient, I enjoyed seeing him and Caleb together. Largely surrounded by a ward full of women and babies, Martin seemed to enjoy having a guy —a dad— to hang out with. He seemed perfectly content to sit on the bed next to his grown-up friend and protector. They talked, read and played quiet games together.

Despite whatever trauma Martin had experienced in his early childhood, Caleb's nurturing attention was a healing balm.

And Martin did heal.

Of course, the medical staff did their part; it's their job, and they do it well. But I am convinced the relationship between Caleb and Martin which developed over those weeks at Kijabe Hospital was the game changer in Martin's life.

In a secular setting, we might call Caleb a social worker, but at the Mama Grace Home where he works rescuing street boys, he is a Godsend.

One of the sad realities of urban Africa is the

great number of boys under age twelve who live on the streets. Some of the boys are abandoned by their parents, some are kicked out of their homes and some run away.

In the final grim picture, it almost doesn't matter which terrible reality made a child homeless. The end result is the same—a child alone, hungry, vulnerable, easily exploited and hard to rehabilitate. We needn't think long to uncover some of the evil and lawlessness boys experience when the street is home.

I never heard the events leading up to Martin's being found and saved. By the time he entered my world at Bethany Kids Children's Hospital, he was a bandaged boy with a loving, protective and kind guardian.

When he leaves the hospital, he will begin life under Calebs's watchful eye at Mama Grace's Home. Martin will have homework, household chores and loving discipline. He will attend public primary school and weekly church. If advisable, steps will be taken to reunite Martin to his parents.

Sometimes restoring a boy to his family is problematic, if not ill-advised. In fact, Martin's mother was the reason he was there. She had soaked his hands in gasoline and lit them on fire. His mother was arrested, charged, convicted, sentenced and imprisoned for her actions against her son.

This is the reason Martin is homeless.

I don't know if it was an isolated instance, or the last straw of a long, short life of abuse.

What was his offense?

Was he being punished for misbehavior?

Was he caught stealing, touching, or breaking a forbidden household item?

It doesn't really matter. Nothing would justify the horrific suffering inflicted on him by his mother.

So there she is. The guilty mother.

So there he is. The victim child.

So here we are. The bystanders, the appalled, the self-righteous.

So there is Caleb. The advocate, the peacemaker, the bridge, the evangelist.

So there is God.

"He will not always accuse, nor will he harbor his anger forever; he does not treat us as our sins deserve or repay us according to our iniquities. For as high as the heavens are above the earth, so great is his love for those who fear him."

It remains to be seen whether Martin will ever be restored to the care of his mother. But God, who does not change, can change water into wine, cause the blind to see, the deaf to hear and the lame to walk. He can turn a heart of stone into a heart of flesh. He heals the broken-hearted and binds up their wounds.

Pray for Martin's healing: His healing hands, his healing spirit and his healing memories.

Pray with Caleb: pray that each of us, having discovered and lived God's plan for our lives, may finish strong. "I have fought the good fight, I have finished the race, I have kept the faith. Now there is in store for me the crown of righteousness which the Lord, the righteous Judge, will award to me on that day—and not only to me, but also to all who have longed for his appearing."

Maranatha

Come, Lord Jesus

EIGHT

The Woman Without a Name

I AM THINKING of a woman whose name I don't
know. Nor do I know her child's name. I don't know
why she was in Bethany Kids Hospital, except that
she must have had a sick child.

All I do know is that whenever she saw me, she
beamed.

She would get a glimpse of me down the hall,
turning into a room or going out the door, and she
would smile. Her face registered the recognition.

Her chin lifted, her lips parted and then the
reward: a radiant, glowing smile. Her mouth opened
wider as if to speak. No noise came out, but it looked
as if she were saying, "Hey!"

If her hands were empty, which was not usually
the case, she would wave. It was not a wave of "Stop!

I want to tell you something." But just recognition, a salute even.

It was, "Hey, I know you!" Or more to the point and more important, "Hey, it's me! You know me!"

But sadly, I didn't know her then, and I don't know her now. I still don't know her name or her child's name, or why they were at Kijabe. I didn't know then, and I don't know now if the child was gravely ill or is fully recovered and waiting to be discharged.

At one point I could have solved this mystery. The first time I realized the inequality in our "friendship," I could have fixed it.

"I'm sorry, help me out here... I have forgotten your name."

But no, I didn't do that. It would have been too embarrassing for me. I would have to admit that I mess up, that I'm not perfect after all. I. I. I. I. Me. I. I. Me. I. I. I.

But no. (Here I go again.) I didn't do it. Pride won.

One nanosecond of humility and I could have avoided the prolonged, unresolved discomfort of a missed opportunity to do the right thing.

If I am ever in this situation again, will I have learned from my mistake? There is nothing much sadder than a missed opportunity to do the right thing.

NINE

Abigale

SHE RAN GIGGLING down the Bethany Kids Hospital corridor, looking more like a Reggae musician in a Jamaican night club than the mother of a hospitalized child.

Although mothers of pediatrics patients are required to wear the standard issue, frumpy pink hospital gown, Abigale's sense of exotic fashion and fun prevailed.

Technically she did wear the gown, but covered it with a layer of colorful fabric, tied like a sarong at her waist. Another African print cloth was artfully wrapped around her head, completely covering her hair and framing her animated face.

Truly, all she lacked to complete the look was a straw hat festooned with tropical fruits. She was a small woman, with flashing big eyes and a brilliant smile of perfectly aligned, dazzling white teeth.

She ran after me, flagging me down and interrupting my rather sedate routine of chatting with and praying for patients and their mamas.

"Come with me to see my child! My bebe, come see my child!"

She stopped just short of running me down. Instead, she skidded to a stop, giggling and crashing into her friend. By now, the friend was giggling, too, perhaps even a little embarrassed to be drawn into the scene unfolding in the pediatric ward.

"Can you come with me? My bebe needs prayer!"

"Of course, I will pray for your baby. First let me finish seeing the mamas in this room. Then we will go." I tried to grant her request without adding to the circus she was creating.

She had an idea. "Oh! I will meet you there!"

As she turned to bolt out the door, I called her back.

"Wait, I don't know your room number!"

"My bebe! My bebe is in the ICU!" she shouted triumphantly. "No, wait!" Big smile. "I will take you. I will wait. I will sit right here and wait." Looking around the room at the other mamas patiently waiting for prayer and reassurance, she did wait... for about seven seconds. Then she jumped up. "Can we go now?"

This whirling dervish of a woman-child took my breath away. I had many first impressions, but the strongest was an incredulous, "ICU? That girl's baby is in the Intensive Care Unit?" I tried to sort my thoughts as they piled up inside my head. "This girl is crazy! Has she any idea how sick her child is? Is she in denial?"

She went scampering ahead while her friend and I tried to keep up, taking two left turns, going up a ramp, past the security guards and some maintenance workers. We passed through hallways lined with patients awaiting outpatient services, clinics of one kind or another, patients in their pink gowns, hobbling down halls with their new crutches or wheelchairs.

This little fireball greeted patients and staff alike with wide grins, winks, quick handshakes while calling out greetings and well-wishes to all. She was like a politician soliciting votes from unlikely constituents. It was quite a scene watching her work the crowd.

Hustling behind, trying to catch up with her, I felt as if I was taking a walk with a Labrador Retriever puppy.

Finally, we reached our destination. Abi was right. Her baby was in the Intensive Care Unit. Several patients, including her infant daughter were there, alive, but barely so. Only two visitors are allowed for each patient, so her friend took a seat in the hall.

As she and I prepared to go in, I began to witness

the most amazing thing: she was being transformed before my eyes. She quietly adjusted her tousled head scarf and shifted her skirt around so it was straight. She showed me where we were to wash our hands.

Then she paused. A long pause.

Her big smiling eyes had changed. Not sad, but serious. She looked older.

She paused again and lowered her head. She pursed her lips, then relaxed them. Then she looked up and held the door open for me to enter the ICU.

Her baby, Purity, was in the last bed on the left. A nurse was tending the baby. Checking tubes, wires, monitors, she was efficient and gentle.

Looking up and seeing the baby's mother, she nodded and spoke in Swahili. The nurse's voice was soft and reassuring. She gestured to the various leads secured with adhesive to the tiny chest. She pointed to the place where the surgeon had made a tiny incision to allow access to her heart. Explaining one thing and then another, the nurse treated the baby's mother as a respected member of the team.

Mama listened, blinking with interest and understanding.

Abigale never got to touch her child. She didn't ask and was not offered the opportunity. She just stood, sharing the space where her baby lay and listening intently to every word of the kind nurse.

Still in the ICU, surrounded by the hums and beeps of modern medicine, she looked over at me. Seeing the tears form in my eyes, she turned to comfort me and took my hand.

"I know God will heal my baby. I had another baby. My other baby died. He had pneumonia and died. I know God will heal my baby."

TEN

Lap of Luxury

TWELVE HOURS AGO, I was being noisily bounced around like a bean bag in a clothes dryer. This pounding was the final torment of thundering around lion country in the back row of a seven-passenger open-air Safari vehicle on a deeply rutted road, with rocks the size of basketballs. All this on an empty stomach, with a full bladder and no idea of "how much longer 'till we get there."

When we finally "got there," back to our room and in one piece, Don mentioned something about the upcoming game drive, conveniently scheduled for 6:30 the following morning.

In response to that news I chose my words carefully, but unmistakably.

"There is no way I am EVER getting back in that safari vehicle."

So, this morning he is there, and I am not. I am here, lounging on our elegant four-poster bed, which is artfully draped with mosquito netting, and sipping outrageously delicious Kenyan coffee with steamed milk, delivered to our "tent" by a uniformed steward who wonders if there is anything else he can bring the lady.

I have to admit, one reason I was so able to blow off today's morning game drive is that, on the whole, yesterday's game drives could never be topped. The sights we saw were incomparable.

One of several memorable events began as we saw a mother cheetah resting, while her two cubs frolicked nearby. Just spotting a female cheetah with two cubs is enough to reward our guide with a sizable tip.

But the adventure was just beginning.

While we watched, she gathered the little ones and began to stalk an impala. The cubs followed her and we followed the cubs. Other animals in the vicinity stopped grazing and turned their attention to the mother cheetah. Undetected to us, she somehow told the cubs to stay put. At once, they both "sat" and "stayed."

In our safari vehicle, we stopped talking and sat still, too.

Mama cheetah shifted her attention in another direction, and after a pause, she took off like a shot to bring down a small gazelle. Her cubs didn't move. Once the gazelle was down, the cubs stayed put, but we followed her.

With considerably more noise and less grace, our safari vehicle bounded cross-lots over the grasslands and came to a halt about fifteen yards from an open space where she was guarding her fresh kill.

We could hear her panting in exhaustion as she waited about twenty minutes before calling her cubs to her side. She made a soft mewing sound. At fifteen yards, we could barely hear it, but the cubs, still several hundred yards away, got up and joined her for the feast. Within minutes of the cubs' arrival, two buzzards and a jackal arrived to clean up the leavings.

We were speechless at the drama we had just witnessed.

Indeed, much of life seems to boil down to being at the right place at the right time. That was certainly the case for us this day. Our good God pulled back a curtain for us to see the cruel and beautiful everyday life of wild creatures, including the powerful animals exploiting the weak and defenseless.

We unarmed spectators responded with silent fascination and even pity. And resignation. The life of one is paid for by the death of another.

Has it always been like this? Was it like this before the fall of humanity, indeed the fall of the whole world? Sin and death were introduced into the world in a garden, a place so like the scene of our drama today.

Do we, like the cubs, so easily move from care-free frolic and entertainment to stealth and slaughter?

Are we and our "advanced" civilization little more than those animals grubbing for a place on the food chain, seeking to use others, even the misfortune of others, for our own survival, comfort or advancement?

How long does this go on?

In the end, when Jesus returns, will He not put all things right?

The lion will lie down with the lamb. The wealth and comfort of one people will not depend on the poverty of another. He will judge between the nations and will settle disputes for many peoples. They will beat their swords into plow shares and their spears into pruning hooks. Nation will not take up sword against nation, nor will they train for war anymore.

But there still exists that one death, the one that is on behalf of the rest. The necessary death, the substitutional death of the One for us all.

Maranatha.

Amen.

Come, Lord Jesus.

ELEVEN

Jonah

———————

"My name is Jonah and I love Jesus!"

A bold proclamation for a man from such a closed society as the Maasai. He was a big man. He was not dressed in traditional Maasai regalia, but a polo shirt and jeans. He appeared to be in his fifties.

I responded to his forthright manner in a similar fashion, making eye contact and reaching out for a firm and friendly handshake.

We hit it off immediately. Ignoring the patient he was there to see, he drew me into small talk, speaking a little loudly by hospital standards.

But Jonah was not alone. He was accompanied by, and also ignoring, a timid woman who appeared to be about his age. She possessed none of his self confidence or good humor. He did not introduce me to her, but I took her hand and gently squeezed it. She responded, but with a great deal less enthusiasm than one might consider polite.

"Masai women lead more secluded lives than men," I thought, "maybe she's just shy."

Meanwhile, the baby slept, and the lovely young mama looked on.

I tried to figure out the cast of characters assembled in the room.

At first, I thought maybe the older couple were new grandparents, father and mother of the mysterious and silent young woman seated on the bed. Then I paused and considered another possibility. Jonah might be the father of the baby. He was clearly in his fifties and the young mom only about seventeen. That's quite an age difference, but culturally permissible.

But then, what about the older lady? Was she the baby's grandmother? No way! She sure wasn't acting like any grandma I ever met! She acted bored and even disapproving.

But maybe... what if... the older lady was the head wife of the older gentleman. If Jonah is the patriarch of a large Maasai clan, then maybe the young mom is his third or fourth wife. In that case, the older lady is likely to be a senior wife who has taken this journey with her husband to bring the junior wife and her new baby back to the clan.

That is all conjecture, but what happened next was equally puzzling.

Jonah left the room to tend to bill-paying in the business office. This left the mysterious, silent young mom, her baby, the annoyed, sullen older lady, and me sitting in the room. I busily made lame, one-way chatter about something or other, not knowing if either woman had a remote clue as to what I was blathering on about.

The older woman started to fiddle with her earring. Like all Maasai women, she wore heavily beaded, intricate jewelry. Her dangling earrings were diamond-shaped, solid with multi-color beads, from which hung metal discs on each of three small chains. The earrings hung down about two inches to the level of her chin.

She continued to finger the earrings, and I realized she had removed one. Then the other. Then she stood up and walked across the room and handed the earrings to me. She almost smiled.

"For me?" I pointed to my own chest.

She put her hand over mine and held it to my chest.

"I can't take these. They are beautiful."

I spoke with somewhat exaggerated gestures and vocal inflection, thinking, *This is crazy! I can't take your jewelry!*

Pause. "Thank you, but no. I can't take this."

I returned the earrings and backed out of the room, knowing that was the wrong thing to do, but too shocked to do anything but remove myself.

Just outside the room, in the hospital hall, I paused again.

Leaving wasn't the answer. The earrings were a gesture of friendship. We will probably never meet again. But she wanted to remember me, and wanted me to remember her.

How could I refuse her?

I returned to the room.

Standing in front of the older woman, I removed my own silver earrings. I handed them to her. She smiled and once again gave me her earrings. Trade accomplished, we both smiled.

I easily put her earrings in my ears and shook my head to feel and hear the light clinking of the metal discs. Both women giggled at my delight over this beautiful and most unexpected gift. After a close inspection of the goods, the young mom helped her senior put my earrings in her ears.

We stood looking at each other, pleased with our trade. We hugged and said goodbye.

TWELVE

Naomi

————————

AFTER SEVERAL WEEKS, I had come to see the Bethany Kids pediatrics ward as a kind of bizarre sorority house. Many of the pediatric ward Mamas were away from home for the first time. Some had never left the village where they were born.

Despite the hardship that brought them together, there was joy in their laughter, encouragement in their girl talk, and always compassion. These "sisters" had in common the shared experience of caring for a sick child.

It was understood that some children would be discharged to home, where they would join the family and grow to adulthood.

It was also understood that some Mamas would go home with empty arms and a broken heart.

One particular day, I noticed that although all the beds were occupied, the ward was unusually quiet. Babies nursed, toddlers napped and Mamas quietly entertained their littles.

But there was no singing. No laughter. No telling stories about home and family.

I missed the chatter and giggles I had come to expect and enjoy.

As I entered the ward, the first bed on the right was made up for use. Three women: an elderly lady, a middle-aged lady and a young woman sat on the bed. They sat in silence with their backs turned to the others. Next to the young woman, a tousled bundle of pink blankets snuggled a new arrival.

"Good morning, ladies," I ventured. They all looked up, but only the young one made eye contact with me. For that reason, I focused on her.

"I don't believe we've met." Pause. "My name is Elaine, and I'm a volunteer here."

Nothing.

Thinking to myself, *Shy? Not all three of them! No English?*

Speaking a little slower and trying again, "Are you new here? When did you come to Kijabe Hospital?"

Finally, a response! The young lady said simply, "We came yesterday."

"Well, we are so happy to have you here!" Followed by my peppy cheerleader smile.

"We are leaving today. We are discharged."

I was still pushing for some small talk, some explanation. "Oh, that's wonderful! Such a short stay. I'm glad you can be on your way home with your new baby."

The young mother responded with appropriate words, although it seemed a little "off."

"Yes, we came yesterday and saw the doctor. He said we could go."

I plowed on. "Well, a short stay is a good thing, isn't it!"

"Yes."

I couldn't figure out why this conversation was so weird. Every new mom likes to show off her new baby, and I'm pretty good at fawning over newborns, so why wasn't this working?

Pressing on, I said, "Well, before you leave, can I take a peek at the baby? I won't bother you if she's sleeping, but there's nothing cuter than a new baby!"

The young woman left the baby on the bed but reached over to touch the bundle. In one movement, she pulled back the blanket.

The anticipatory smile on my face froze. I stared,

trying to make sense of what I saw in the blanket. I caught my breath.

In the span of a second I silently chastised myself for being an absolute and complete idiot. Why didn't I take every clue she gave me? Why did I have to keep talking?

Too many words then.

No words at all now.

Idle chatter failed.

Still half smiling, I took a breath. I tried to recover.

Nothing.

There was nothing I could say to comfort the sweet, grieving mother who looked to me for all the reassurance she had not gotten from her mother and grandmother sitting next to her.

Reassurance that she could do this. She could love this child. She could raise this child in a community that thought she was cursed for having the child, and the child was cursed for being born.

Reassurance that she had not delivered a monster.

Reassurance that God still loved her, and God loved this child.

Collecting myself, I spoke slowly and reached to

stroke the baby's soft cheek. "Oh, what a wonderful baby. Look at those eyes... That sweet mouth."

And a moment later, recovering, looking into the Mama's eyes. "What have you named your little girl?"

THIRTEEN

My Last Good Cry

ON DAY ONE in our Kijabe house, the first time I sat on the bed, I laughed out loud. It was, without a doubt, the hardest, most rigid, uncomfortable, unforgiving mattress I had ever felt.

Don said it was "firm."

So I laughed some more. Then my laughter turned into tears, and I cried. Even at the time, it seemed like a silly overreaction, but I couldn't stop. It was like a warning, a chastisement: "Don't look for comfort here. Life here is hard, and you will cry."

Yes. And still.

I cried for silly things: the cupboard door that wouldn't stay shut… and the one that wouldn't open.

I cried for the oven that would callously and

mysteriously turn itself off in the middle of a baking project.

I cried for Don's unfailing delight in this adventure, knowing that my daily struggle was the only thing keeping him from enjoying it to the fullest.

I cried for Matthew, the maintenance worker cleaning the garbage cage. I never saw Matthew again. This is not that big a place. Was he an angel? Was he sent to open my eyes to the heartbreaking nobility and beauty of serving God in the hard places?

I cried for James, who lives in one room with his mother and two brothers. One day he reached for a kerosene lantern, bringing it closer so he could study his schoolbook. But the lantern spilled and doused his body with flaming kerosene.

I cried for Leah, a young woman who sells bread door to door. She wants to go to school, but her mother and sister died of AIDS, leaving her to care for her sister's three young children and her father, while he dies of AIDS.

I cried for Hannah, who traveled from a city 600 miles away to bring her son to Kijabe Hospital. The world turns its back while al-Shabaab terrorizes her community in Northern Kenya, going door-to-door murdering her Christian friends just because they are Christians. Hannah and her husband defy the threats and continue to teach Somali children to read.

I cried for Caleb, who cries for the little boy he saved from the streets, the child with his hands bandaged like boxing gloves because his mother soaked them in gasoline and set them on fire. Now Caleb visits the child's mother in prison and teaches her about the love and forgiveness of God.

I cried for the fallen humanity that Jesus died for. That such a death was necessary only because all our good works, all our righteous acts, all our good intentions are filthy rags compared to the endless love and compassion of Jesus. My work was nothing. I listened and prayed and cried. Only Jesus saves.

I marvel at ten weeks in Kijabe without one day of illness. The headaches and back pain that nag me at home never materialized. Mysteriously gone.

I marvel at the night sky with the constellations in place and the moon so bright it casts a shadow.

I marvel that, for all the brokenness, heartache, disappointment and uncertainty, my friend, Amani, can say, "God is good. He is so good. I thank Him for bringing you here to this place, my friend. He is so good. When can you come back?"

FOURTEEN

The Dream

———————————

Last night I had a dream.

MY HUSBAND and I had been camping. Our canvas tent was pitched in the desert. There were no other people in sight. No other tents or signs of life. Really, nothing but our tent.

We were preparing for a trip. It was just a day trip. We left our baby in the tent with the girl and started walking.

After a time, we returned to the tent. As it came into view, it looked so small from a distance. I had thought of it as quite spacious, but from this vantage point I could see its silhouette barely stood out against the wide horizon. When we paused to rest, a man appeared and said there was food in the next village, and we should go now or there would be none left.

But there was the baby. I needed to take care of the baby. I walked closer, listening for sounds of life coming from the tent. I heard nothing. No baby cooing or crying. No young girl talking, reading or singing to the baby.

Standing in front of the tent, I didn't want to pull back the flap. By now the silence had convinced me the baby was alone, if she was there at all. My thoughts came at once and in no particular order:

How long had the girl been away?

And what about food?

Had she gone to the next village for food?

Didn't I leave any food for the baby?

And water?

No, I don't think I did.

How could I leave a baby in the desert with no water?

I pulled back the tent flap. It was heavy, but it let in a shaft of light. The tent was for protection, yet it was hotter inside the tent than outside.

Relief. The baby was just as I had left her.

But when was that? Today, I hoped. Surely, I wouldn't leave her for more than a day.

Well, maybe two. At the most, three...

I knew I should go to her, but I held back.

"I'll wait until she moves. Then I'll know she is alive."

When she moved her foot, I walked over and picked her up. The baby had dark brown skin, which kind of surprised me. Had she been brown all along?

I only had white babies. Four little white, bald baby girls. They are all grown up now. And now this little brown baby with curly hair.

I tried to nurse this baby, as I had nursed the others. But like Abraham's Sarah, I was well past the age of nursing babies.

That became a moot point as I found the baby was too weak to nurse, too weak to even try.

How could I have let this happen? She was my responsibility and I had left her. I had left town with my husband for God-knows-how-long and left her in the care of a stranger. A girl whose name I couldn't even remember, and now she, too, was gone.

5:00 a.m.

When I woke up, I did not want to open my eyes. Even knowing it was all a dream, I still kept my eyes closed. I had to stay with the baby; I couldn't abandon that baby again.

Acknowledgments

Even a modest effort of publication is the result of many people's influence and labor. To these people and organizations I owe sincere thanks.

Thank you to World Medical Missions (the medical arm of Samaritan's Purse) for allowing us to serve in Kenya five times, These experiences have changed us in too many ways to count.

Thank you to Kijabe Hospital for opening your doors to us and allowing us the privilege of serving your community.

Thank you to Christ Community Church and our small group. Your interest and encouragement have reminded us we are not alone in this endeavor.

Thank you to our partners, Gary Eggleston, M.D., Tim Gorman, M.D., Tim Kitchen, M.D., Lorie Lashbrook, M.D., Matthew Wehr, M.D., and staff of West-field Family Physicians. In our absence you carried on the work of the Great Physician, skillfully and lovingly meeting the medical needs of those entrusted to our care.

To my husband, Don, who never stopped believing my stories should be shared.

Also, thank you to Terry Mosher, Stefanie Tessmer, Ryan Burrows, Justus Marete, Laura Anderson, Kate Karyus Quinn, Marilyn Hall and Rebecca Hartwig. Each of you has played an important role behind the scenes in bringing this experience to life and to print.

Thank you to our daughters, Heidi Kaminski, Jill Jordan, Joy Sonju and Laura Anderson. You were with us for the first missions trip to Kenya in 1987. It was you who made it the most memorable and life-changing event of our lives together. You continue to delight us every day and in every way.

Finally, thank you to Bethany Kids Children's Hospital. I was honored and challenged to volunteer at Bethany Kids for even a brief time. The work you do with sick and disabled children across Africa is nothing short of magnificent. Daily your medical teams save lives, bringing health and healing to their young patients, all in the name of Jesus.

ELAINE BRAUTIGAM LIVES with her husband, Don, a Family Physician in Westfield, New York. Since 1987, this group of missions-minded doctors and their spouses have rotated time off to volunteer their services in underserved parts of the world.

Elaine was born in Memphis, TN. Due to her father's career, the family relocated to a new city every few years. When Elaine was 10, she had a friend whose father never got transferred to a new city. This sounded pretty good to Elaine. But her friend's father was a doctor and often on call, frequently missing parties, family dinners, special events and school functions. For that reason, Elaine declared to her mother that she would never marry a doctor. She almost kept that vow. But in 1973, she married Don Brautigam, a third year medical student.

Elaine received her education at Syracuse University where she received her B.S. and M.S. in Speech Communications.

Elaine and Don have four daughters, four sons-in-law and seventeen grandchildren.

CPSIA information can be obtained
at www.ICGtesting.com
Printed in the USA
BVHW041215151121
621687BV00014B/841